Frédéric Delalot

washingtonias and zoetropes
4

KDP Editions

Between the rows, light

Climate concentration

So eras...

Here and there...

After several years

Like an ether...

The interlude was there

Temporal...

We'd see...

We were trying to become...

Towards the ice...

Holographic...

And we were regaining the Coast

The formats seemed to be available

Blurry punctuations...

A few moments...

Invisible, in front of me...

Perspective...

Size...

Sudden pleasures...

Of sentences, progression.

Cycle restarted

Of a different order...

Historical...

Robust...

In bohemia, invited a memory ...

Dazzled by enjoyments...

There was in the evening the possible scent of things

There were many insatiable ways...

The nightlife, fast...

You were naked, infinite freedoms, the century was long

There was a hypnotic scent there...

Memories mixed their arches...

Blinds half closed crossings ...

Well before the end of the party...

Many fall asleep, life stretches

Summer, at the heart of the stories...

I thought: later...

She went to the other room

Oasis, sensation, computers

Historical novels

And those of the back-to-school season

She was moving fast...

Between the rows, light...

Immensity of things...

Strength to opt for an attitude.

Pavement of a building...

Which became possible to reproduce

Climate concentration...

Incredible trade, accessories...

Lingerie

Shoes

Expression orbit

Corporeal, strange

Paint the town...

Participate...

Guess...

At first glance...

Young people go out...

From toe to toil...

From nothing to ease

Since the Renaissance...

Physically...

Intellectually

Everyone loves each other...

Had a drink...

Or went to bed...

Resort area...

So eras...

Her era and another

More remote...

Silent...

For an outside eye

Suburbs of Paris...

Like a series

Possible...

Here and there...

Purple pouf...

The cat was falling asleep...

We were moving

In this space...

Naked, plane...

She loved sales.

In the summer darkness

After several years...

There was the fish-man

I had heard of

At the Cité...

Tapas, doors

From a sedan...

On the waves...

This century...

Claims

Heady...

Our privacy.

Actually...

He knew...

Good addresses

She let him...

We had traveled Manhattan

Again, like no one...

Ship of languages, descent...

Zigzagante, at the back...

Without insisting too much...

Witnesses of the cold...

In the heart of a forest

From Seine-et-Marne...

Integrate...

About ourselves

Surprising...

Like an ether.

I got up early

On weekends...

Complete...

Giant canvases...

Which smelled like the dragee...

Narrow triangle deck

In a corner...

She wanted more...

The interlude was there.

Proud of me...

Temporal...

And simple desire...

Moments of symbiosis

During an evening...

We hope to have access to it...

This breath of fresh air...

Shows up only once

Continual back and forth

Continue creation...

Of four large...

Scenographic...

She would paint...

We'd see...

Next charm

Passers-by...

The star...

From the night...

This century...

Symphony

We were on the massif...

Limestone, faded...

The machinations of silence

In the suburbs...

Parliaments...

Insomniacs...

Under the fanfares

And the rain...

In a remote time...

By the harbor of dreams

Immutability...

We were trying to become

Neglecting the appearance...

Whimsical...

Excess...

Sensual...

Overhanging.

Dance...

Oily body

The interlude...

Towards the ice

The River...

Boats

A hundredfold...

Mirages...

Ink...

Dunes...

White...

From the old world.

Which revives...

Mires...

These turrets...

From where we would be passengers

What to do with the mysteries?

The black trees...

Frank memory...

An Icelandic diatribe...

Crossroads...

Night...

Upstairs...

Spheres

Holographic

The darkness...

Yews and lilacs...

From Persia...

And we were regaining the Coast...

To the overflowing vials...

Beyond the purple clouds

Where the gates brought us to the rides

The insurmountable dream...

Where innocence ends...

Seeming to appear...

Crossing the border

From a wood...

Quintessence...

Abusive peace...

I was praising the lion...

Prepared for semester

So unreasonable...

Stands out the moment

Which indulges...

Of a silence...

Seeing it, always...

And she had dreamed...

From the planet...

The formats seemed to be available.

The pines...

This impression...

Heterogeneous...

Exhaustive sum

It seemed to me...

Vermeille, purple

Blurry punctuations

Gave us an air

Land in zones...

Invaded by roads...

The sunniest...

From its waiting alcoves

Had sufficed...

Bibliophile images

Cliffs of the ocean...

Memorable suites...

Velvet...

Abstruse, luxurious

A few moments

Sunk...

Crossing the border

Quintessence...

Abusive peace...

In the wave...

We mixed.

Invisible, in front of me...

A poster, my past

My experiences...

Distant horizon...

Which supports everything...

The manna...

Humans, under the sky...

Storm remembrance

Find Attention

Beneficial rays

The permanence...

White sentence...

Innocuous wanderings...

Hypnotic will...

Unattainable, the barge...

Reflections, another time

Virgin night....

And the time comes

So unreasonable...

Our speed...

Perspective...

From a cell

Unique, emerald...

Amphibious...

Sequence...

Towards a different universe

Influence of evolution...

Invincible by nature...

Size...

Hypervolumes

I had wanted to...

Pass...

Intense field...

Prepared for semester

Raw material...

Human activity...

Floating at bedtime.

Invisible, the Cape...

Unexpected, in the distance...

Something is happening...

Ripple, currents of a force

Sudden pleasures

Hours elapsed

Late did not exist

Only faces...

Chance crowds...

These acres of joy...

Beaches, grains of sand...

Of the planet, perceptions.

Same algae...

First rain...

The pride of heights

Depending on shapes...

Sentences, progression...

Practical, constitutes the form

Ultimate, mental tourism

Virtuality to extend dreams

From some units...

That is, jump...

Towards Unity...

I can't find any trace

Between two civilizations...

Nothing, even in the immediate future

Human, nascent...

Over time...

Abandon themselves

Their archives

Mental...

Any multiplicity

Nomad, which was going

Making a difference

Cycle restarted...

Which predisposed...

Infinite serenades.

Like a color

Initial releases...

History...

Of a different order...

Difference...

In humans...

From the First Story

Ancient times...

The imagination...

Calls us...

It comes from far away

Heaven upside down.

On the edge

Lying there...

One hundred sailboats

Stranded...

Knowledge...

Essential basis

Intelligence...

Very fine...

Victory...

Historical...

Comes from afar...

New temple

From the earth...

Tourists...

Sports...

Snowshoes.

The book

Entitled...

Of joy...

Robust...

And healthier

Browsers

Was already winning...

Escaping...

From one of them.

Coming, winner

To His Kingdom

Of colors...

That he had established

He knows that time...

From now on, talk to him

From the capture...

From the world...

We were young, this time...

Nordic charm, evenings of exile...

In Bohemia, invited a memory

Off the narrative, the pond of the park...

In this part of the city center...

The weather was getting drunk, and the autan...

Infinite mirages, and joys...

And the city would be reflected, the feline evening

We superimposed the eras...

It was a never-ending story...

As we were lying down

Dazzled by enjoyments...

Black mini-skirts in imitation leather...

In the summer, I passed between fountains...

We arrived there, infinite terrace...

Uninhibited, entertaining possibilities

Escapes, eternal hope...

To understand, and we wanted

A bit of the Sonata of Vinteuil...

Under tall trees...

11

And I would have remembered a summer in Gruissan

The narrative gained in retrospective clarity...

Ah! we wanted, we wanted...

All the beauties of the world

In the memory of the years

Hadn't we already wandered...

And made these journeys...

There was in the evening the possible scent of things...

We were walking around Old Montreal.

There were unreal worlds...

How many possible moments...

Sand clouds, flying papers

And time sculpted realities

Drowsiness...

Leaves were flying...

With hours, days

And the nights were ticking, the summer...

From our dreams of the day before...

Coach rocking our memories...

The old town was relaxing...

There were many insatiable paths.

How many posters

After a few sleepless nights...

On the heights of Florence...

Osmosis evenings are exchanged

Until nightfall...

And hope, this light...

As for a caressing party

The nightlife, fast...

Ah! I had found vinyls

Of Alphaville, rebirths...

We were going out in the night...

We were going to have drinks...

And we were regaining the Coast...

Near the rocks of the Fig tree...

Beginnings, dreams through the streets

The foliage, the virginity of the evening...

12

This is where we relate to life, between sheets...

The suns of an islet were rushing, perhaps...

During our nights, exotic trophies, pleasant route

Sometimes hope, image loading speed

Long nights, pensive, liquor of happiness

Carried by the sails of the imagination...

Hours from the coast, I see the nights of a summer...

You were naked, infinite freedoms, the century was long...

Let us not postpone the enjoyment of the moment until tomorrow.

Between two books, the look towards the horizon

Mesmerizing spheres, piles of novels

Words, in the background, from other pages

Summer was coming back, yesterday's adventures...

Finding you, love of all the suites

Which reigns, around, masts of the boats...

There was a hypnotic scent there

In the evening, motionless sailboats, that summer...

Kind of a crown, we wouldn't know until later

Baroque pages, intercourse, small beaches...

And foreigners passing through danced, undressed...

Wet necks, loop of restarts...

By the Conservatory, filiform muses...

We were taking the unforgettable road...

And we invited happiness to join us

Sublimated sensations, singing of the waves...

Truce in Paris, as stopover...

Memories mixed their arches

Roses, chimerical unfolding...

Made by my thoughts...

Material unfillment...

A thousand nights, a million years...

Million years, at least

Being able to touch all things

Euphoria in the drunken night, infinite

At the peak, the snow was doubling

We talked with nomads

Heavenly improvisations...

One evening in June, flowing dress...

Half-enclosed blinds of the crossings

Caresses of the coasts near Brighton...

I had to change my mind a hundred times...

Comings and goings, along the brush

As we dreamed...

And I had preferred to love our frolics

We would see each other again, attracted...

Eternal drunkenness of the cities...

In these possible escapades

Because I gave myself time

To appreciate the atmosphere...

It was the heart of the time...

This latitude of noumènes...

I was passing by a chapel

Well before the end of the party...

And I could hear music...

The blank page was rushing

Always triumphant...

Gave us America

In the corners...

Many fall asleep, life stretches...

Copper sea, in Old Montreal...

The story we continued...

Like those conspicuous trips...

Telling the thread of life...

It was already writing the dream...

Like that, I envied you

My senseless nights...

From top to bottom...

I put on a t-shirt...

Parallel to dimensions

I was so different

On the edge

Of a happiness

Adventure...

Prospects...

When the hours are discussing...

Passion, as we dreamed...

With plans, absolute innocence

Lettered thoughts

Under a vault...

Capital, there...

Something alchemical...

Young adults from ancient times

Summer, at the heart of the stories...

A moment, unspeakable trances

These years, I had loved them...

Illusions, we all crossed paths...

Between sequences...

In our thoughts...

Preparatory...

Speeds during the summer...

Hours Transformation

From America

Momentum...

Hourglass...

Azure...

Years that I replaced...

More slender, depending on the location

Like a processor...

Flashback for a moment

The capitals there...

Slow liners, a thousand years old

Dimensional journeys...

He enjoyed the moment...

Perhaps it is futile to understand

In the evening, exhilarating jubilation, liberating

All day, in a mall...

So many moments...

The century...

In the bubbles...

Limits of the ordinary

Summer...

15

Creative moments, rolled up sheets, festive fatigue

Towards mesmerizing horizons, almost purple...

Quick street tours...

Symphony...

Of a silence...

In the corners

Life stretches...

Heady...

Avenue du Levant.

Away from the stations...

Little by little, whimsical...

Like those conspicuous trips

Telling the thread of life...

The interlude...

I envied you my nights

From the old world....

I put on a t-shirt...

Parallel to dimensions

Squarely on the edge of...

Happiness, adventure...

To the overflowing vials...

Mountain, with plans...

Thoughts in lettering...

So unreasonable...

Summer, at the heart of the journeys

Star of the night...

In the suburbs...

Parliaments...

Slopes of ecstasy

From this place...

Between sequences

These films...

Immutability...

Speeds...

During the summer...

Overhanging...

Rather America.

16

Myself

Elk...

Hourglass...

Azure...

More slender...

Depending on the location

Like a processor

Spray bays...

Capitals of there...

Magnetic...

At the end of the wanderings...

Dimensional travel

He enjoyed the moment...

Free suite...

Insurmountable dream

The mist dissipated

Drunk sheets, I was reading

Unless all the impulses

Have been repeated...

Fog of an era...

White night, blue angels...

There was music...

Where only faces existed

Coming back in the evening, at night...

Between two districts...

Around a Mont...

From a cross planted...

I remember...

We went with others

Rue de la Roquette...

Crystal, calendar tour

Azure, invincible spheres

In these streets, bohemian...

This troupe...

Light walks...

That was a very long time ago...

A term of reflection, perhaps.

17

The air traveler, unconscious...

Peloponnese, red sand...

Place in a few frescoes

Light houses, white cities

Of words, planetary interests...

Library gardens...

I loved snow days...

In the meantime, caresses of thought...

I saw graffiti between the towers.

Impression of feelings...

From Reims or elsewhere, I read...

We had been students, designers

A little ardor...

Chance, as they say...

Many years would pass

Our loves, nascent feasts

From Brighton, on the lake...

Vaulted cellar...

Party, music...

Multiple meeting

On the street...

Sometimes slow...

Behind...

On street lamps

There is a whole sky...

We finished a few evenings

At that time, forever rites

Percussion is accelerating...

Legendary corridors of spaces

Miniatures...

Of joy...

Of a few dreams

Off-text...

Order of things, time...

Apparently, in its purest form...

Transported us...

We were together, apart.

18

Multitude

Full of unknown journeys

Imbued with emotion

Presumably shifted heat

I didn't want to rush anything...

Decades passed...

Eternity, garden, anchor point...

In the park...

Flower headband, weekend.

Villages of rapprochements...

I remembered a hotel...

From Saint-Paul Street...

We were talking about spherical villas

After some Spanish hostel

By ear, guardian of the world...

Sheltered numbers...

Sailing school in the sun...

After the rain, they walked...

Above multiple crossings...

Images inhabited me on occasion

Standing, desert by the sea...

Then we slammed the doors

Fullness, illusion, indefinite din

Metamorphosis in the white sky...

Between the trees, horizons...

When the world was asleep

In the present of the Earth

Years passed...

Sensitive taverns...

After seasons...

To the Square...

Servers-volleyball players

Curvatures, gravitation

Passages...

Caravans...

Realize...

Transition.

19

All at once

Destination...

Almost wise...

We crossed paths

In Phillips Square...

New thought...

Which was watering us...

Near the caravans...

I fell asleep late.

Intoxicating coat...

Real, years

Ark of the world...

At the borders...

Terraces...

America...

Cliffs...

Asphalt mist

I stroked her skin...

In an instant, curvatures

Gravitation, passages...

Silver shores...

All this...

Warmth of possibilities...

The dawn had seemed immense

Transported us...

We could see the city

Inner courtyards

Between the blinds...

This theatre...

It was jumping out of the mists...

Raising the paperwork of dreams

Suspended from this boom, movements

Bohemians, in the past...

At the edge...

Expanses

Elegance

Tiny...

20

Postal appearance...

Only accessible

By swimming....

Attraction...

From those moments

From an era...

Hypnotic feelings

And we had peace...

Those summers...

Eternity of embraces...

Without chains

Sailboats...

Plots of stories...

It was no time...

Drifts...

Hopes, snow at dawn

Behind the Illusion...

Infinite cycles...

Yielding to the heavens of dreams

Multiple colors...

At that time...

Describe the universe

Platforms

Hours wasted

Fortuitous mirages...

On the other side of the spectrum...

Collective memory...

Geniuses, rhythms...

Giants, on this sphere

Maybe we're getting attached

Many times, like our alcoves...

Statues in a square...

Time differences...

The heat occupied us with happiness...

More disconcerting...

Atmosphere, décor of shelves...

Whose origin we did not suspect.

21

And you can't write anything...

Subtle apparitions...

Miniature of joy, of summer

Gigantic paintings...

Then, the modeling takes place

With every illusion...

We didn't ask ourselves any questions

Blissful retreat, somewhere in July...

At the end of the eighties...

So many images, sequences...

Reversed, scattered disorders...

Entanglement of immutability

Ancillary decision-making forums

Already taken, laugh together...

Because of a memory, perhaps...

Believe in the impossible, perhaps...

With the seasons, which bring everything

Pines, extraordinary rock...

What do we spy on in the night...

Which wonders, nothing else

Than a mysterious stay...

Unknown waves...

Which started we don't know where

And we prowled around...

Streets still unknown...

It was the unknown which guided them

In the distance, like a color...

Chance, as they say...

After the wandering of the city...

She was going to the other room...

Described wide circles...

Transcended hours passed

The future was there...

After the trees...

Appointment...

That we thought they were random

To have fun...

22

And we saw their present

Representations...

Or future images...

The weather was getting drunk...

And the sea, and her breath...

Euphoria in the drunken night

Infinite, at the climax...

Hours from the coast...

I look back on the nights of a summer.

The story we continued

Marine, overlooking...

There was music...

We were talking about villas...

Spherical...

At that time

Reconciliations

Of festivities...

Emerging...

And I tap my watch...

Elastic, living present

Perverse instrument, ideal.

Wandering, getting ready to steer your bezel

Towards the celestial vault, boreal hemisphere...

I continue straight ahead, frantic scrambling...

Coming from the neighborhoods, marc of a bottle ...

Ready to ride, in Florence...

Iconic weekend...

One winter, we are talking about romance...

Vestiges, time is strewn with milestones

She remembers her departure...

Alchemical stimulation, sensation

To live, and the moment, the rhythms...

Gothic rejoicing...

At the border, to settle...

Then, in a cycle country...

The excitement of departures...

And I'm crossing new boundaries.

23

By the furrows of life...

Towards the door of the Opera...

I ran every year

Curious screamers who wondered...

We were nipping, we were each other...

The drunkenness of orgasm, automatic metropolis

Abundant ornaments

Attention chapardeuse

Between constructions.

Harnessed motorcyclists chatted...

Pink radio, transparent, which would whisper...

There, we have these relaxing corners...

In height, when we become nomads

Inviting, without compensation...

Receptacle of imagination...

To save myself from millennia

From the gigantic tangent...

Which slides in slow motion...

Across contrasts

Within this area...

Puff of days...

Order of emptiness...

In the company of tesserae...

So many times, best tries...

With this reality, country of coasts

Virtual armadas, little by little

The stage of the Republics...

Dust from modulated forums

Hot headlines on the surface...

Bourgeois countryside...

The sea, rival, on one side

On the one hand, ardent...

At the tail of the stanzas...

Square...

Which stirred me up...

When I was twenty years old

Methodical journeys...

24

I didn't even tell the time anymore

We are invisible energy...

Celebrating a brightness...

Epic paintings on the walls

The true color of chance

Not far from the world...

The size of a man...

The universe, an inexhaustible source

The sea, its schooners...

The heart of imaginary frescoes

Unusual sails, finally, I see...

The Empire at its peak...

In Paris, all these conjunctures

Knowing well that they are the ether...

New peoples, movements...

Through the faded windows of a bus

Which had brought me to this neighborhood...

Dishes on the go, others to delight me ...

Auvergne omelettes, endless streets...

Flights of birds, stairs coaxed ...

Our desires, formerly, this happiness of an Anse.

The hypersonic air of the offerings...

Electronics zest of the Earth...

From a pressed orange, we were building...

Fortifications, a story, unexpectedly

I quite like drunkenness

From the night, where the words

In cloud, we inhabit

The values themselves...

That we defended...

Extremely logical...

Which separates us from the dawn

There are Atlantean days...

The nascent adventure soaked our embraces

From a travel oil, we hesitated...

To erase the tough dreams, the hopes...

Old grunts, the inexhaustible enthusiasm...

25

Long periods of introspection...

Desires turned towards innocuous roads...

Had this energy, the beautiful part of recharging

The climate intermediary

Rope of habits...

Contours of consciousness

Freedom, beginnings...

The basics of the Order

At the call of the clouds...

Behind the fountains

Of materials...

There was a shortcut

Present of trophies...

Sensual power...

According to the sensations...

Randomly, almost...

Outside, the frightening open sea

Distinguishes a few words...

Drifts of pages, books

Almost at the same time...

By one of these coincidences...

I put away the manuscript

Hesitant kilometers...

Which clung to each other

In the century of clothes

We were getting closer...

With the attraction for infinitude

And joy, temporary distance...

Looks like laurels...

What do the statues carry...

Power plants in a square

We're heading there...

Fantasies glimpsed...

Nights passed, thus, in a second

Words sculpted by clouds, rushes...

I remember, with this doubt...

What does hindsight provide, unnoticed...

26

Currents that stammered sensational returns

The fluid of propulsions, in the afternoon, the shadows

Branches, turned the eras, in the distance ...

And the open landscapes, the dispersals

We created, stopping at the essentials...

At independences, try to choose...

A title, hardly writing...

Short booklets, dominating a Zen court

With long and indomitable impulses...

In order to live more...

I have this pleasant road...

The immense wave of time

In the sea of space...

These are rites, at night...

A universe of cliffs, the ocean...

Memorable suites, illuminated...

Sap of ancient times, getaways

Maybe it's not just that...

Maybe she's the one who dreams of colors...

Regular artifact scenes, juxtapositions

Lights, little by little, on the snow, sun...

Activities, coats

We never got tired...

To go around the ages...

I want to read again, to write

A few sentences of time...

As in the park, the lounges...

We look at the objects, the pieces

Shore of the St. Lawrence, streets of Paris

On the Coast or elsewhere...

As we were gypsies...

Outside the bubbles...

Where does the arena align

Like the desire for black waves...

To approach the coasts, these summers

We need parentheses...

Color of hyperwords, hope...

27

We had an entire report...

Pinnacles, with new eyes...

Reborn earths, fluid fabrics

At the end of the blank images...

I had boarded with a trunk

Once, misty castles

In the roll of tables...

Diabolos, a remote era

Immediate, other tracks...

End of the possibilities

In the form of words

And exchanges...

Status quo, displays...

Sliding between the curtains

Or the red drapes...

Casting a comet look

Instead of a story...

With the ease that magnetizes...

And I heard, by the thrill...

Drowned from the branches...

A techno diatribe, Icelandic.

Absolute, exclusive...

Spirals...

A wave in the present

Floating in the ether...

Words stolen from darkness...

I had gone on a trip...

White paper size

Skateboarding thinking...

Waltz of hours...

There were big streets

Between carefree walls

Between schedules...

Lights in slats of the blinds...

Around the abundances, the flowerbeds...

That we capture by circulating with our eyes

On my side, I had a track...

The Platform of the Republics

Hunted the ordinary...

Eyelid flapping...

Mischievous, immodest light...

And it attracted our smiles...

Insomniacs, imbued spaces

When their embrace lasted...

Timeless clothes...

To any destination.

Crazy lands lightly...

Our annual concerns...

Outside, visual symphony

Of our negligible stirrings

Through a sarbacane...

The bastions of the day before yesterday...

Constantly reborn, aerobatics...

We were considering the rest of the story

Tourists with bare legs

Glow of our hearts intact

And it will look the same

In cadence, out of time.

I erased the figures of the years...

That I replaced with a page...

Irreplaceable fauna of Paname...

Which was soaring, insatiable, baroque

Experiments, of the time

Exaggerated, it emanated an energy

Protruding from a rocky picture...

Caught up in flight, first fruits...

From a fanfare...

Character reflections

Which crossed paths...

There was a reality

Next to the eras...

To the brim of watches...

Virtual machine...

Quiet, garden style.

29

Particular anarchy

Findings of yesteryear...

In this flood of ideas

Some remains...

Remained hooked

Above the trees

Forms of their Empire...

Eloquent signs...

Encryption in stone.

That's right, that was what they felt...

The indefinable charm, clinging to this dream...

To this ideal, which fed us with so many images

Sequences, things, wills...

They were the time...

Dynasties, Temporal Order

Art and speech, these years...

Pretexting a curiosity...

The beginning of a gush...

With letters, flexibility...

The lightness of the drifts...

One era taking away another.

Somewhere, high hopes...

It was like the crazy gallop...

Horses, along the beaches...

Antiques, at the height of taboos

I saw Paris in yellow squares...

Oranges or almost purple...

The reservoir of money, our cadences

Still drifting, America...

The image of the flowerbeds...

Getting drunk, free freedom...

Once again, terrace...

Primal time out of the blue

Our steps, wide omnipresent

We are in the moment

Gameplay, fervent...

Walking towards the horizons...

30

Luminous prints...

From our wandering thoughts...

Spain's scorching roads

After the reeds, a few months

Illuminated windows, lapses, ribbons...

We were adding to the mergers

Exhilarating limits...

For smoother empires

Joining us with the blurry air...

Floors, a ship...

Correlated particles...

Between the spheres of the sea

I surprised a glimmer...

Their precious nature...

Formatting work...

Along erotic spaces

There were the peasants...

From the corner, the terminals...

Romans, to be conquered

Every sigh...

We were going astray...

A temporary distance...

Looked like laurels...

What do the statues carry...

We could hold with the stars

This impression of sublime

Every mirobolant fantasy

In the square, we were freed...

From the outset, rehearsals...

Palm trees, frimes of circumstances...

Providing donations, free passes

Inspiring desires, comptoirs du Sud

Until the hugs, I dragged ...

Geometries...

Variables...

Like a lamp

Magic...

Light...

Field

Astrolabes

We were already free...

And this latitude continued...

Forms of the planet, its attractions

Fickle diagram...

Pine cones...

Semillant centers.

I started from an illusion...

Of a fleeting impression...

Then redundant...

In a square of squirrels

Paths, often...

Circus of stories...

From atmospheres to wanderings

Asking slow suggestions

I was going to accompany this dream...

Antique, exhaustive sum...

Couldn't we hear the notes

From a superior organization...

The nations of luck...

Appealing to articulated images

Collect a bag of hours...

I like that part...

Already the basis of our start-ups

And we prowled around...

When bodies attract...

The engines are silent...

Overlays of realities...

Shifted by depth...

Possibility of metamorphoses

From this transmutation...

Like that, in brewing...

Fortune of links, luxury of things...

Let us only touch, new days

Constantly hero of the slightest unreason...

Color of hyperwords, hope...

In the past, misty castles...

Slipping between the curtains...

That we capture by circulating with our eyes

Timeless clothes...

We were considering the rest of the story

Experiments, of the time

Above the trees...

The lightness of the drifts...

The reservoir of money, our cadences

Illuminated windows, lapses, ribbons...

Between the spheres of the sea...

Every mirobolant fantasy...

Shapes of the planet, its attractions...

To the pose of slow suggestions...

Fortune of links, luxury of things.